43 Natural Skin Cancer Meal Recipes That Will Protect and Revive Your Skin:

Help Your Skin to Get Healthy Fast by Feeding Your Body the Proper Nutrients and Vitamins It Needs

By

Joe Correa CSN

COPYRIGHT

© 2016 Live Stronger Faster Inc.

All rights reserved

Reproduction or translation of any part of this work beyond that permitted by section 107 or 108 of the 1976 United States Copyright Act without the permission of the copyright owner is unlawful.

This publication is designed to provide accurate and authoritative information in regard to the subject matter covered. It is sold with the understanding that neither the author nor the publisher is engaged in rendering medical advice. If medical advice or assistance is needed, consult with a doctor. This book is considered a guide and should not be used in any way detrimental to your health. Consult with a physician before starting this nutritional plan to make sure it's right for you.

ACKNOWLEDGEMENTS

This book is dedicated to my friends and family that have had mild or serious illnesses so that you may find a solution and make the necessary changes in your life.

43 Natural Skin Cancer Meal Recipes That Will Protect and Revive Your Skin:

Help Your Skin to Get Healthy Fast by Feeding Your Body the Proper Nutrients and Vitamins It Needs

By

Joe Correa CSN

CONTENTS

Copyright

Acknowledgements

About The Author

Introduction

43 Natural Skin Cancer Meal Recipes That Will Protect and Revive Your Skin: Help Your Skin to Get Healthy Fast by Feeding Your Body the Proper Nutrients and Vitamins It Needs

Additional Titles from This Author

ABOUT THE AUTHOR

After years of research, I honestly believe in the positive effects that proper nutrition can have over the body and mind. My knowledge and experience has helped me live healthier throughout the years and which I have shared with family and friends. The more you know about eating and drinking healthier, the sooner you will want to change your life and eating habits.

Nutrition is a key part in the process of being healthy and living longer so get started today. The first step is the most important and the most significant.

INTRODUCTION

A varied and healthy diet will provide you with the necessary vitamins and nutrients to keep your immune system strong and will reduce the risk of skin cancer. Making a few small changes in your diet will increase your bodys capacity to fight skin cancer.

Some studies recommend at least 35 weekly portions of vegetables, including broccoli, radish, tomatoe, cauliflower, and kale. Also, dark green leafy vegetables like spinach, beet, leaves and collard greens should be part of your everyday nutrition. The reason is that these foods contain a large number of powerful antioxidants and various bioactive substances that will decrease the risk of melanoma.

Because of the anti-inflammatory benefits found in foods high in omega-3, which can be found in fatty fish, it's a good option to include these great foods atleast into one meal minimum a week.

43 NATURAL SKIN CANCER MEAL RECIPES THAT WILL PROTECT AND REVIVE YOUR SKIN: HELP YOUR SKIN TO GET HEALTHY FAST BY FEEDING YOUR BODY THE PROPER NUTRIENTS AND VITAMINS IT NEEDS

1. Radish Hero

Description:

Radishes contain Vitamin C and antioxidants, which makes them quite effective in preventing skin diseases and inflammation. Regular inclusion of radishes in your diet results in healthy and radiant skin. Steamed radishes have a very tender and delicious taste

Ingredients:

- 20 radishes
- 2 tbsp water
- 1 tablespoon olive oil
- salt and pepper to taste

How to prepare:

- Trim the ends off of the radishes and peel a band of radish-skin from around the middle of the radish.

- Steam the radishes in a covered microwave safe container for 8 minutes, or until fork tender, serve immediately.

Nutritional facts:

Calories:109 Fat:11.6g, Carbohydrate:1.5g, Protein:0.4g

2. Asparagus the Great

Description:

Asparagus is an excellent source of anti-oxidants and it also contains a group of substances collectively called the saponins, known for their anti-inflammatory effect. Research has shown that these two work in concert to reduce stress. Stress, which is a lot more than the usual "stress" that people feel mentally, is not a healthy scenario for people developing cancer.

Ingredients:

- 1 pound of asparagus
- 1 tablespoon olive oil
- unrefined sea salt and pepper to taste

How to prepare:

- Trim asparagus, this is easily accomplished by snapping the ends off where it snaps naturally.
- Pour olive oil over asparagus and toss to coat.
- Season generously with salt and pepper.
- Put on a hot grill (medium heat) and grill until

asparagus is tender (turning often), about 5-10 minutes.

Nutritional facts:

Calories: 112.2 Fat: 7.5g Carbohydrates: 10.3g Protein: 5.2g

3. Mount Chestnut's Soup

Description:

Research has shown that sweet chestnut offers antioxidant properties. One study examined sweet chestnut's ability to inhibit free radicals and found that its antioxidant potential was at least on a par with that of quercetin and Vitamin E

Ingredients:

- 3 tablespoon olive oil
- 1 medium carrot, finely chopped
- 1 celery rib, finely chopped
- 1/2 medium onion, finely chopped
- 2 cups cooked chestnuts
- 1 cup ruby port
- 1 thyme sprig
- 3 cups chicken stock or low-sodium broth
- 1/2 cup heavy cream
- Salt and freshly ground pepper

How to prepare:

- Add the carrot, celery and onion and cook over moderately low heat, stirring, until softened, about 10 minutes.
- Add the chestnuts and cook for 4 minutes.
- Add the port and thyme and cook over moderately high heat until the port is reduced by half, about 4 minutes.
- Add the stock and bring to a boil. Cover partially and simmer over low heat for 30 minutes.
- Discard the thyme sprig. Add the cream to the soup. Working in batches, puree the soup in a blender.
- Return the soup to the saucepan and bring to a simmer. Season with salt and pepper and serve

Nutritional facts:

Calories 345, Carbohydrates 9.6g, Protein 8.4g, Total Fat: 30.1g

4. Bavarian Salat

Description:

This is like a German potato salad served warm, and it's definitely one of the tastiest. This salad may be made a few days in advance and brought to room temperature before serving.

Ingredients:

- 4cups potatoes, peeled and sliced 1/4 inch thick
- 2cups chicken broth
- 1cup bacon, chopped
- 1/2cup onion, minced
- 1teaspoon sugar
- 2tablespoons lemon juice
- 1tablespoon Dijon mustard
- 1/2cup flat leaf parsley, chopped

How to prepare:

Place the potatoes and stock in a small saucepan and bring to a simmer. Cook until the potatoes are tender but still retain their shape. Drain the stock, reserving some.

While the potatoes are cooking crisp the bacon in a skillet. When it is browned and crunchy pour off and reserve the bacon fat. Reserve the crisp bacon. Whisk together until smooth the lemon juice, sugar, Dijon and 4 tablespoons of the warm bacon fat. Toss with the potatoes, onions, crisp bacon and parsley. Add a bit of the reserved chicken broth to moisten if needed. Season to taste with salt and pepper. Cover and let rest for two hours at room temperature before serving.

Nutritional facts:

Calories: 318.9 Cholesterol: 24.4 mg, 729.9 mg, Carbohydrates: 31 g Protein 10.3

5. Cheesy Broccoli Soup

Description:

Broccoli sprouts are a particularly rich source of cancer-fighting compounds, but also broccoli florets provide significant amounts. To maximize the benefits of broccoli, eat it raw or slightly steamed. Consumption of raw, crushed broccoli has been shown to result in faster and better absorption of the cancer-fighting compounds in broccoli. Cooking can destroy up to 90% of sulforaphane — the key anti-cancer substance in broccoli.

Ingredients:

- 3 tbsp potato starch
- 3 tablespoon olive oil
- 1 small sweet onion, diced
- 2 stalks of celery diced
- pepper to taste
- 6 cups chicken stock
- 4 cups chopped broccoli
- 2 cups whole organic milk, coconut milk, or raw

milk
- 3 cups raw shredded cheddar cheese
- ¼-1/2 tsp freshly grounded nutmeg

How to prepare:

- In a stock pot, saute onions and celery until tender (about 5 minutes).
- Add in potato starch and stir.
- Add chicken stock to stock pot slowly while whisking.
- Stir in chopped broccoli and simmer over low heat for 30 minutes.
- Stir in milk and cheese and allow to heat through (about 5 more minutes).
- Serve with some shredded cheddar cheese.

Nutritional facts:

Calories: 261.1 Fat: 16.5g Carbohydrates: 13.8g Protein: 15.2g

6. Epic Banana Bread

Description:

This bread is perfect for breakfast or for snacking. Banana is great not just for skin, but one's overall health as well. There are many powerful nutrients contained in this fruit that make it the perfect addition to your daily meals.

Ingredients:

- 6 organic eggs
- 2 ripe organic bananas mashed
- 1 tbsp raw honey
- ⅓ cup melted coconut oil (cooled)
- ½ tsp unrefined sea salt
- ½ cup coconut flour
- ½ tsp baking soda
- ½-1 cup chopped raw pecans or walnuts

How to prepare:

- Preheat oven to 350 F.
- In a large bowl combine eggs, honey, and the cooled coconut oil and mix well.

- In a small bowl combine coconut flour, salt, baking soda and stir well.
- Add dry ingredients to wet ingredient (except banana) and stir until there are no more lumps.
- Fold in bananas until well blended.
- Pour batter into 2 greased mini bread pans or 1 5"x9" loaf pan.
- Bake for 40-50 minutes or until lightly browned

Nutritional facts:

Calories: 165.8 Fat: 12.8g Carbohydrates: 9.4g Protein: 4.4g

7. Carrot's Cake

Description:

Carrots are also an important vegetable to include in your diet if you are worried about developing skin cancer. Because of their high beta-carotene content, carrots are great at protecting the skin against harmful ultraviolet radiation from the sun. Make carrot into cake and even kids will love it.

Ingredients:

- ¼ cup coconut flour
- ¼ tsp sea salt
- ¼ tsp baking soda
- 1 tsp ground cinnamon
- 3 large eggs
- ¼ cup coconut oil
- ¼ cup raw honey, more to taste if needed
- 1 tbsp vanilla extract
- 1 cup carrots, grated
- chopped walnuts and raisins, optional (If adding

raisins, no more than ½ cup, and if adding walnuts, I'd keep it to around ¼ cup chopped and some to sprinkle on top of frosting.)
- Cream Cheese Icing
- 1 6 oz pkg. softened organic cream cheese
- 1 tsp vanilla extract
- 1 tbsp of raw honey
- ¼ tsp sea salt

How to prepare:

- Preheat oven to 350º F.
- Combine all ingredients and put in greased muffin pan ⅔ full. Note, if you want the muffins big, you might only need to fill 8 muffins ⅔ full.
- Bake for 18-24 minutes. Insert a toothpick, when it comes out clean it is done.
- For frosting combine cream cheese, vanilla, honey and salt and 3 tbsp of water and whip on high speed for 3 minutes.
- This will create a fluffy and smooth frosting. You can put the frosting into a small plastic bag and

cut the tip of a corner off and pipe it onto a cooled carrot cake cupcake.

Nutritional facts:

Calories: 155 Fat: 11.1g Carbs: 10.3g Protein: 3.3g

8. Easy Sorrel Salad

Description:

Some of the health benefits of sorrel include its ability to boost eyesight, strengthen the immune system, improve digestion, build strong bones, increase circulation, increase energy levels, help prevent cancer, reduce certain skin conditions, lower blood pressure, increase appetite, slow the aging process, protect against diabetes, strengthen heart health, and improve kidney health. Sorrel is a fascinating perennial herb that is used all around the world and is cultivated for a wide variety of uses. Although it is primarily grown for use in food, due to its sharp, tangy taste, it also has a vast array ofhealth benefits associated with it.

Ingredients:

- 1/4 cup whole-milk yogurt
- 1 tablespoon extra-virgin olive oil
- 1 tablespoon fresh lemon juice
- 1 tablespoon minced shallot

- 1 tablespoon finely chopped fresh chives
- 1 teaspoon sugar
- 1 avocado
- 1/2 teaspoon Dijon mustard
- 1/4 teaspoon salt
- 1/2 pound sorrel, coarse stems discarded and leaves torn into bite-size pieces (4 cups)
- 1/2 pound hearts of romaine, torn into bite-size pieces (4 cups)
- 1/4 pound frisée, trimmed and torn into bite-size pieces (2 cups)
- 1/2 cup loosely packed fresh flat-leaf parsley
- 2 tablespoons loosely packed fresh tarragon, leaves coarsely chopped if large

How to prepare:

- Whisk together all dressing ingredients in a large bowl.
- Toss together all salad ingredients with dressing in bowl. Season with salt and pepper.
- Cut avocado into cubes

Nutritional facts:

Calories: 215, Carbohydrates 15g, Protein 7g, Total fat, 2.9g

9. Roasted Happy Seeds

Description:

A quick snack available for anyone, especially for our kids. Easy to prepare and lasts for a long time. Vitamin E is very essential for a healthy skin and this anti-oxidant is present in pistachios. It integrates the cell membranes of the mucous membranes of the skin membranes. It protects skin from harmful UV rays, prevents from skin diseases and makes skin healthy and more beautiful.

Ingredients:

- 2 cups shelled pistachios

How to prepare:

- Preheat oven to 350 degrees F.
- Spread the pistachios evenly on a rimmed cookie sheet. Place in the oven for about 6 to 8 minutes They will become very fragrant when they are done.
- Remove from oven and transfer to a plate immediately.

- If you want to remove the skins from the pistachios place them on a clean towel and rub them. The pieces will slide right off. It's easiest to do this when the pistachios are warm.
- Let the pistachios cool and then you can store them.
- They taste amazing in baking recipes when they are toasted.

Nutritional facts:

Serving Size: 1/4 Cup, Calories: 170, Fat: 14g, Carbs: 8g, Protein: 6g. **Vitamin A10% , Vitamin C11% Calcium12%, Iron26%, Vitamin B-6104%, Vitamin B-120%, Magnesium 37%.**

10. Futuristic Veggie Chips

Description:

Oven-fried zucchini chips taste like they're fried, yet they are baked and amazingly crispy. These chips make a healthy substitute for French fries • Zucchini is rich in Vitamins A and C as well as antioxidants which can benefit your skin in many ways. Regular consumption of zucchini helps restore the moisture of your skin, providing you with aglowing skin.

Ingredients:

- 3 small zucchini, sliced into ¼- inch rounds
- 2 tablespoons olive oil
- ½ cup Italian seasoned bread crumbs
- 2 tablespoons grated Parmesan cheese
- 2 teaspoons fresh oregano

How to prepare:

- Preheat oven to 350 degrees F (175 degrees C).
- Place zucchini in a bowl. Drizzle olive oil over zucchini and stir to coat; add bread crumbs and

toss to coat. Spread coated zucchini onto a baking sheet. Sprinkle Parmesan cheese and oregano over coated zucchini.
- Bake in the preheated oven until zucchini are tender and cheese is browned, about 15 minutes

Nutritional facts:

1 Serving (10 chips) Calories:92, Total fat: 2, Carbohydrates: 14, Protein: 6, Sodium 340mg

11. Old School Yogurt

Description:

The health benefits of yogurt have always been important to mankind. Yogurt is a powerhouse of various vitamins and minerals that are also present in milk. Furthermore, yogurt is a good source of easily digestible proteins. Yogurt is beneficial for maintaining cholesterol levels in the body and preventing ailments like hypertension, while also boosting immunity. It is good for improving the strength of bones and teeth, aids in digestion, and is valuable in skin care.

Ingredients: (2 cups)

- 2 cups raw milk or raw goat's milk
- 2 tbsp full fat organic yogurt (one that has live active yogurt cultures in it)

How to prepare:

- Place 2 tablespoons of organic plain yogurt (full fat) in a clean glass pint size mason jar. Once you make your yogurt, you can use 2 tablespoons of your fresh raw yogurt in your next batch.

- ext you want to heat your raw milk to 105ºF-115ºF. This temperature is low enough that the nutrition and enzymes of the raw milk are not lost.
- Once heated, remove from heat and stir in about 1/4 cup of milk into mason jar with yogurt. Stir well. Add remaining milk and stir until all combined. Place the lid on the mason jar tightly. Wrap mason jar in a thick towel and place in the oven (the oven is not turned on, it is used as an incubator) and turn the light on to offer a little heat. Leave in oven for 24 hours.
- After the 24 hours your yogurt will look like this. Homemade yogurt is a lot thinner then store bought yogurt. This is a normal consistency. If you want it to be thicker you can strain your yogurt by simply draining the liquid out through cheesecloth or a fine mesh sifter/strainer. This liquid is the whey. Whey can be used as an acidic medium when soaking oats or grains.

- Refrigerate your yogurt for 2-3 hours before serving and it will firm up slightly.

Nutritional facts:

Calories: 169.4 Fat: 9.3g Carbohydrates: 12.6g Protein: 10.2g (1 cup)

12. Roasted Organic Kohlrabi & Sweet Potato

Description:

Sweet potatoes, one of the oldest vegetables known to man, are one of the most nutritious vegetables and contain plenty of nutrients with skin cancer fighting properties. Fresh kohlrabi stem is rich source of vitamin-C; provides 62 mg per 100 g weight that is about 102% of RDA.Vitamin C (ascorbic acid) is a water-soluble vitamin, and powerful anti-oxidant. It helps the human body maintain healthy connective tissue, teeth, and gum. Its anti-oxidant property helps the human body protect from diseases and cancers by scavenging harmful free radicals from the body.

Ingredients:

- 1 cup cubed sweet potatoes (skin removed)
- 1 cup cubed kohlrabi (skin removed)
- 1 tablespoon olive oil
- 5 sprigs of fresh thyme
- salt and pepper to taste

How to prepare:

- Mix all ingredients together and roast in a 450 F oven for 25 minutes, turning half way through the cooking time.

Nutritional facts:

Makes 2 cups, Serving size is 1

cup Calories: 176.8 Fat: 11.5 gCarbohydrates: 17.0

g Protein: 2.1 g

13. Fresh Summer Organic Salsa

Description:

Avocados are brimming with nutrients that are thought to reduce the risk of skin cancer. Avocados top the list of the best dietary sources of glutathione, an important antioxidant.

Ingredients:

- 2 tbsp organic olive oil
- 1 tbsp fresh lime juice
- 1/4 cup chopped cilantro
- 1/4 tsp unrefined sea salt
- 1/4 tsp freshly ground pepper
- 2 cups fresh non gmo corn, cut off the cob (about 4 ears)
- 2 avocados diced into 1/2" pieces
- 2 cups cherry tomatoes, quartered
- 1/4-1/2 cup finely diced red onion

How to prepare:

- In a large bowl, whisk together the olive oil, lime

juice, cilantro, salt and pepper.

- Add to it the corn, avocado, cherry tomatoes and red onion.
- Stir gently and serve at room temperature.

Nutritional facts:

Calories: 206.2, Fat: 15.1g, Carbohydrates: 18.9g, Protein: 3.6g

14. Organic Guacamole

Description:

Avocados are the main ingredient in guacamole, a popular and healthy food commonly used as a sauce, spread or dip. Avocado contains vitamins D, A and E, which all help to smooth skin tone and soften skin. The essential oils in avocados also have been shown to reduce the appearance of age spots and improve sun-damaged skin. These benefits occur when avocados are eaten or when they are applied directly to the skin.

Ingredients:

- 2 avocados halved, pitted, and removed from peel
- ½ tsp salt
- ¼ tsp pepper
- ¼ cup fresh tomatoes, diced up
- ½ of a lime, juice squeezed out, about 1 tbsp
- 2 tbsp fresh cilantro, chopped
- 1 tbsp red onion (optional)

How to prepare:

- Combine all ingredients and mash with fork.
- Serve immediately.

Nutritional facts:

Calories: 148.9 Fat: 13.4g Carbohydrates: 8.5g Protein: 1.8g (¼ cup)

15. Organic Fruit Splash

Description:

Strawberries are super fruits, bursting with powerful anti-oxidants and loads of vitamin C that will provide your skin with nourishing nutrients for healthy happy skin. Avocados are brimming with nutrients that are thought to reduce the risk of skin cancer. Make together into salad and benefit your skin!

Ingredients: (Serves: 4 servings)

- 2 avocados peeled and pitted chopped
- 1 cup strawberries finely chopped
- ½ of jalapeno minced, seeds removed
- 2 tbsp chopped cilantro
- ¼ tsp ground cinnamon
- 1 tbsp organic olive oil
- lime juice from ½ of a lime
- ¼ tsp unrefined sea salt

How to prepare:

- Mix all the ingredients together and gently stir.

Nutritional facts:

Calories: 226.8 Fat: 18.8 Carbohydrates: 15.4 Protein: 3.7 (1 serving)

16. Veggie Noodles

Description:

Craving Thai Food, but need a Raw, Vegan alternative? This pad Thai recipe is almost easier than calling for take-out. It'll make your head spin it's so fast and delicious. This meal would provide an excellent source of vitamins and nutrients.

Ingredients:

- 2 zucchini
- 1 carrot
- 2 green onion
- 1/2 cup mushrooms
- 1/2 cup cauliflower
- 1/2 cup mung bean sprouts
- 2 tablespoons sesame oil
- 1 tablespoon lemon juice
- 1 t garlic
- 1 t ginger

How to prepare:

- Use a spiralizer (or mandoline, or peeler) to create your noodles. Add in veggies of your choice then top with the sauce. It tastes even better after it sits to soak the flavors the next day.

Nutritional facts:

Serving Size: 369: Calories: 208, Total Fat: 14.4, Sodium 957mg, Protein 7.1g

17. Popeyes' Secret

Description:

When it comes to the best foods for preventing skin cancer, it is difficult to beat the superfood kale. This relatively unknown member of the cabbage family is a superhero vegetable cram-full of skin cancer preventing nutrients, including vitamin C and beta-carotene (kale contains 10 times the beta-carotene of broccoli). As a result of its high content of vitamin C and beta-carotene as well as a number of other antioxidant phytonutrients, kale is at the top of the list of vegetables with the highest ORAC rating ORAC, or Oxygen Radical Absorbance Capacity, is a measure of the total antioxidant power of foods. Kale can be eaten raw, for example in salads. The hearty green leaves of kale can also be transformed into a savory side dish by sautéing them and adding onions, garlic and a drizzle of olive oil.

Ingredients:

- ¼ cup uncooked quinoa (rinsed)

- 2 tablespoon olive oil 1
- large clove of garlic (minced)
- 1 cup fresh spinach
- 1 cup fresh kale
- 2-3 tsp lemon juice (start with 2 tsp, and if you would like more add another tsp)
- 2 tbsp raw sunflower seeds or raw pecans (chopped in small pieces)
- ⅓ cup raw shredded parmesan cheese

How to prepare:

- Rinse your dried quinoa several times (this will allow it not to be bitter).
- Boil your quinoa in salted water and cook for 20 minutes.
- Drain and rinse in cold water, set aside.
- In a large skillet add olive oil and garlic.
- Toss your garlic for about a minute and then add your kale and spinach.
- Cook several minutes to wilt your spinach and kale.

- Add your quinoa, lemon juice and parmesan cheese.
- Cook for 2 minutes.
- Toss in your raw sunflower seeds or raw pecans and cook another minute.
- Serve hot or cold.

Nutritional facts:

Calories: 206.6 Fat: 13.8 g Carbohydrates: 15.2 g Protein: 7.1 g

18. Sunset Chips

Description:

Garlic offers a number of skin benefits. Garlic has large amount of allicin present in it and allicin has antifungal, anti-aging and skin smoothing benefits. It is also known to increase antioxidant levels of the skin and body.

Ingredients:

- 1-2 sweet potato, purple sweet potato, russet potato, or red potato
- 1-2 tbsp coconut oil or olive oil
- 3-4 sprigs of fresh rosemary
- 2 cloves minced garlic
- ½ tsp sea salt or more to taste

How to prepare:

- Preheat oven to 400ºF.
- With a mandolin, cut the potatoes as thin as you can.
- Place potato slices in a bowl and drizzle with coconut oil or olive oil (or both) and mince the

garlic and season with sea salt.
- Add the sprigs of rosemary and toss until well coated.
- Place on a broiling pan and bake for 25-30 minutes or until golden brown and crisp.
- If you want them browner, place under the broiler for a minute or two. Be sure to watch them the entire time, they will brown very quickly.
- Allow to fully cool and serve. Store in a paper bag in a cool dry place.

Nutritional facts:

Calories: 150 Fat: 10 g Protein: 3 g

19. Crunchy Coconut Chips

Description:

Due to coconut oil being a saturated fat consisting mostly of MCT's, it will not easily oxidize like polyunsaturated vegetable oils. Most of the skin care products are made of vegetable oils that will oxidize and turn rancid, causing free radical damage to the skin. Often they are made from toxic man-made chemicals.

Ingredients:

- ¼ cup organic extra virgin coconut oil
- 3 cups organic coconut flakes
- ½ teaspoon sea salt (more if you want extra salty)

How to prepare:

- Preheat oven to 300 degrees
- Melt the coconut oil in a jelly roll pan
- Mix the coconut flakes, sea salt in the coconut oil
- Bake a total of 8-9 minutes, stirring every 3 until golden brown. Watch carefully, it browns quickly.
- Pour onto a paper towel – enjoy!

Nutritional facts:

Calories: 200, Fat: 13, Sodium 3mg, Protein 1g, Carbs 1g

20. Organic Potato Boats

Description:

Apart from being used as a food source, potatoes have an important role to play in skincare as well. As pointed out earlier, they are rich in vitamin C which is vital for maintaining skin health. Thus, this starchy vegetable is beneficial for your skin in the following ways.

Ingredients:

- Skins of 4 organic cooked potatoes that are cut in 8 halves (remove the potato from the skins)
- 16 pieces (about a pound) of cooked pastured bacon
- raw cheese of choice
- salt and pepper to taste
- raw sour cream and avocado for toppings

How to prepare:

- Preheat oven to 400F.
- Take your potato skin boats and place onto a pan or into a baking dish.

- Season with salt and pepper if desired.
- Sprinkle 2 pieces of crumbled bacon into each potato half.
- Cover with raw cheese of choice.
- Bake for 10-12 minutes or until cheese begins to slightly brown.
- Remove from oven and serve with some raw sour cream and avocado.

Nutritional facts:

Calories: 220, Fat: 8, Sodium 250mg, Protein 6g, Carbs 31g

21. Garlic's Treaty

Description:

Garlic has a lot of medicinal properties for skin. Its healing elements help the skin to heal and stay smooth and young. Garlic is a potent antioxidant, which helps to regenerate skin and tissues and stay young.

Ingredients:

- 7 large pieces of cubed day old sourdough bread (If gluten free, use gluten free bread)
- 3 tablespoon olive oil
- ½ tsp unrefined garlic salt
- ½ tsp Italian seasoning
- 2 tbsp grated parmesan cheese

How to prepare:

- Preheat oven to 300 F.
- If using fresh bread, cut the bread into cubes and leave on the counter top for a day so it gets stale and a bit hard.
- Place day old bread cubes into a bowl.

- Pour over the bread cubes and toss well so that the bread gets evenly coated.
- Sprinkle with parmesan cheese and toss bread cubes until they are all evenly coated.
- Place on a cookie sheet and bake for 30 minutes, turning them over at the 15 minute mark.
- Allow to cool and store in an air tight container.

Nutritional facts:

Calories: 35, Fat: 2g, Sodium 55mg, Protein 1g, Carbs 5g

22. Pumpkinny Cheesecake

Description:

Beta-carotene (a carotenoid better known as vitamin A), found in the bright orange pulp of pumpkins is known to protect skin cells from oxidative damage caused by free radicals. It is also well known due to its potential anti-cancer, anti-aging and immune-enhancing effects. Pumpkin is also a good source of vitamin C; another powerful antioxidant that combats free radicals.

Ingredients:

Crust:

- 1 cup of nuts of your choice (I used raw walnuts and almonds)
- 4-5 dates (depending on size)
- Dash of sea salt

Filling:

- 2 (8 oz) packages of cream cheese (at room temperature)
- 1 cup of ricotta cheese

- ¼ cup sour cream
- 2 cups of pumpkin puree (roasted from 2 (1 lb)
- pie pumpkins.
- 3 eggs plus 1 egg yolk
- ¾ cup of local honey
- ½ tsp ground cinnamon
- ⅛ tsp fresh ground nutmeg
- ⅛ tsp ground cloves
- 2 Tbsp oat flour
- 1 tsp vanilla extract

Whipping cream

- 1 pint of whole cream
- Honey to taste

How to prepare:

To make crust:

- Grind all crust ingredients in a food processor until crumbly and somewhat sticky.

To roast pie pumpkins: Cut each pumpkin in half, scoop out seeds, place on a parchment lined cooking sheet, Bake at 350 degrees for 45 minutes.

- Allow to cool, scoop out pumpkin and put in a food processor until pureed to consistency.

To make filling: Beat cream cheese until smooth.

- Add pumpkin, ricotta, eggs, egg yolk, sour cream, honey and spices.
- Add oat flour (or arrowroot powder) and vanilla.
- Beat together until well combined.
- Pour on top of crust in springform pan, spreading out evenly.
- Bake at 350 degrees for 1 hour to 1 hour 15 minutes. May still be slightly jiggly.
- Allow to cool, cover with plastic and chill for 4 hours.

To make whipping cream: Whip whole cream in a chilled bowl, add honey to taste (maybe a tsp.).

- Top cheesecake with whipped cream. Sprinkle with fresh ground nutmeg.
- The key with using a springform pan is to well grease the pan and edge around the sides with a butter knife before "springing" it.

Nutritional facts:

Calories: 261.7 Fat: 18.8g Carbohydrates: 19.0g Protein: 6.8g

23. Canadian Garlic Salmon

Description:

New research suggests that twice-weekly consumption of salmon could protect against skin cancer. The high levels of omega-3 fat found in this oily fish are also great for overall skin health; Salmon reduces inflammation as opposed to meat, which increases it.

Ingredients:

- 1/4 cup maple syrup
- 1 tablespoon olive oil
- 1 clove garlic, minced
- 1/4 teaspoon garlic salt
- 1/8 teaspoon ground black pepper
- 1 pound salmon

How to prepare:

- In a small bowl, mix the maple syrup, garlic, garlic salt, and pepper.
- Place salmon in a shallow glass baking dish, and coat with the maple syrup mixture. Cover the

dish, and marinate salmon in the refrigerator 30 minutes, turning once.
- Preheat oven to 400 degrees F (200 degrees C).
- Place the baking dish in the preheated oven, and bake salmon uncovered 20 minutes, or until easily flaked with a fork.

Nutritional facts:

Calories 265 Carbs 14 Fat 12 Protein 23 Sodium 633 Sugar 12

24. Root Juice

Description:

Beetroot is rich in minerals, vitamins and other essential nutrients that keep your skin healthy and glowing. Moreover, beetroot is also very effective in detoxifying your blood and making the skin blemish free and radiant.

Ingredients:

- 1 smallish raw beetroot
- 2 carrots
- 10 French breakfast radishes
- ½ lemon
- 2 apples

How to prepare:

- Cut the segments of lemon away from the skin. Wash the vegetables and chop them into chunks. Core the apples and chop.
- Put everything into the juicer then chill the juice before drinking.

Nutritional facts:

Calories 19, Carbs 5g, Protein 1g, Sodium 45mg, Sugar 4g

25. Fruity Salmon

Description:

Quick, healthy dinner option. Low-calorie for weight loss. Wild-caught Sockeye Salmon is a super food because of its omega-3 fatty acid content. Easy recipe for adding more Omega-3 EFAs in your diet.

Ingredients:

- 1 Pound Wild-caught Salmon, cut into 4 filets
- 2 Oranges, thinly sliced
- 3/4C Fresh Squeezed Orange Juice
- 2T Fresh Squeezed Lime Juice
- 2T Virgin, Unrefined Coconut Oil, melted or Olive Oil
- 1t Lemon Zest – dried or 1T fresh Lemon Zest
- 1T Coconut or Palm Sugar or use Raw Honey or Pure Maple Syrup
- Coarsely Ground Himalayan Salt
- 1/4t Chipotle Pepper or Cayenne Pepper or Chili Powder

- Optional—1 small bunch of fresh Thyme sprigs as garnish
- Optional—fresh Lemon wedges for serving

How to prepare:

Preheat oven to 450º. Slice two oranges into very thin slices, discard ends, and set aside. Squeeze orange and lime with a citrus juicer. Measure out 1/4 cup fresh orange juice and 2 tablespoons fresh lime juice and add to a small glass bowl along with the lemon zest. Whisk in melted coconut oil or olive oil and sweetener of choice, along with salt and pepper. Line a baking sheet with parchment paper. Using a basting brush, brush one side of each of the salmon filets with the citrus mixture then arrange filets on top of parchment paper. Brush tops of salmon with the citrus mixture. Top with orange slices as shown. Brush tops of oranges with the citrus mixture. Optional, wash sprigs of fresh thyme. Tear off a few of the bottom leaves of each sprig. Sprinkle on top of orange slices. Reserve fresh sprigs and top orange slices after cooking and just before serving. Using a coarse grinder, grind some Himalayan salt on top of each filet. Bake 10 to 12 minutes or until salmon is cooked through. Optional—top with fresh sprigs of thyme and serve with lemon wedges.

Nutritional facts:

Calories 275 Carbs 20 Fat 18 Protein 23 Sodium 215 Sugar 8

26. Painted Baby Kale Salad

Description:

The zesty tones of the blood orange and grapefruit segments perfectly complement the full flavours of the earthy beetroot and smooth Gorgonzola cheese in this tasty vegetarian salad.

Ingredients:

For the salad

- 140g baby kale, spinach, or spring green mix
- 200g pack of Juniper berry & Black Pepper beetroot
- 1 ripe blood orange
- 1 ripe grapefruit
- 125g Gorgonzola cheese
- 100g walnut

For the dressing

- 3tbsp olive oil
- 2 tbsp red wine vinegar

- 1 tbsp maple syrup
- 2 tsp dijon mustard
- 6 sage leaves, chopped
- Pinch of salt

How to prepare:

- Wash and pat dry the baby kale; place in a large salad bowl.
- Peel and section the blood orange and grapefruit. Roughly chop the walnuts and beetroot.
- Combine all ingredients with the kale, sprinkling the gorgonzola intermittently.
- Mix together all of the dressing ingredients and drizzle over the salad, tossing until well-coated.

Nutritional facts:

Calories 200, Carbs 10g, Fat 14g, Protein 8g, Sodium 452mg, Sugar 6g

27. Delicious Leftovers

Description:

Researchers found that d-limonene (the major compounds in orange peel) can reduce the occurrence of squamous cell carcinoma, which is a dangerous form of skin cancer. Study participants who regularly consume grapefruit skin, significantly reducing skin cancer rate than just eating the meat alone.

Ingredients:

- 6 lemon peels, cut into 1/4 inch strips
- 4 orange peels, cut into 1/4 inch strips
- 2 cups white sugar
- 1 cup water

How to prepare:

- Place lemon and orange peel in large saucepan and cover with water. Bring to a boil over high heat. Boil for 20 minutes, drain and set aside.
- In medium saucepan, combine 2 cups sugar and 1 cup water. Bring to a boil and cook until mixture

reaches thread stage, 230 degrees F on candy thermometer, or small amount dropped in cold water forms a soft thread. Stir in peel, reduce heat and simmer 5 minutes, stirring frequently. Drain.

- Roll peel pieces, a few at a time, in remaining sugar. Let dry on wire rack several hours. Store in airtight container.

Nutritional facts:

Calories 80, Potassium 69mg, Carbs 16g, Sugars: 15g

28. Healthy Beef's Gift

Description:

Not only does grass-fed beef contain a higher ratio of omega-3 to omega-6 fatty acids (to reduce inflammation), but it also packs nearly 30 grams of protein per 3.5-ounce serving. Protein is the building block of collagen and elastin tissue, which keeps skin taut and less wrinkled.

Ingredients:

- 3 sprigs thyme
- 3 sprigs oregano
- 3 sprigs flat-leaf parsley
- 2 cloves garlic
- 3 tablespoons olive oil
- 1 teaspoon salt
- Freshly ground black pepper
- 1 pound top round, sirloin or filet mignon
- Coarse salt

How to prepare:

- Blend all ingredients except beef and coarse salt

in a food processor.
- Rub on meat; marinate 2 hours at room temperature or overnight in the refrigerator, turning meat once or twice.
- Heat oven to 400°F. Heat a medium cast-iron pan over medium heat.
- Sear meat on all sides until it has a brown crust.
- Transfer pan to oven; roast meat until internal temperature is 120°F, 15 to 25 minutes. Remove; let meat rest 20 minutes (internal temperature will rise to 130°F).
- Slice, sprinkle with coarse salt and serve with Yellow and Green Bean Salad

Nutritional facts:

Per serving: 195 calories (Kcal), 9 g fat, 1.7 g saturated fat, 0.7 g carbohydrates, 0.1 g fiber, 26.3 g protein

29. Veggie-Stars

Description:

Beetroot is your everyday superfood. They are a pretty pink nutritional powerhouse and an excellent example of how food can work as medicine. They are rich in folic acid, iron, magnesium, manganese and phosphorus. The purple-red color comes from betacyanin which is considered an important cancer fighting compound.

Ingredients:

- 250g cooked beetroot dipped in vinegar (not pickled)
- 1 tin butterbeans (410g), drained & rinsed
- 1-2 cloves garlic, crushed
- Small bunch fresh chives, finely chopped (reserve a few for garnish)
- 3tbsp extra virgin olive oil
- Sea salt & freshly ground black pepper

How to prepare:

- Chop the beetroot into small dice, set aside in a

medium bowl.

- In a food processor blitz the butterbeans with the garlic, chives and olive oil. Season to taste with sea salt & freshly ground black pepper.
- Transfer into the bowl with the beetroot and gently fold through to mix. Spoon into a serving bowl, drizzle with a little extra olive oil and garnish with a few snipped chives. Serve as a dip with pitta crisps, or part of a salad lunch spread.

Nutritional facts:

Calories 180, Carbs 6g, Fat 16g, Protein 3g, Sodium 880mg, Sugar 5g

30. Hale Kale Salad with Tomatoes

Description:

This is the basic recipe for a delicious and quick kale salad with tomatoes. You can of course add other ingredients. Kale it's one of the best sources of lutein and zeaxanthin, nutrients that absorb and neutralize the free radicals created by UV light—including the wavelengths that actually get through sunscreen and reach your skin.

Ingredients:

- 1 bunch kale leaves
- 1 medium avocado
- Juice of 1 medium lemon (about 2 cup)
- Dash of cayenne pepper
- 2 teaspoon sea salt
- 2 tomatoes

How to prepare:

- To prepare the kale leaves: glide your thumbnail down the stem, separating the leaf from the stem. Rip the leaves into small pieces.

- Cut the avocado in half lengthwise and remove the pit. With a spoon, scoop out each avocado half onto the kale leaves.
- Add the lemon juice, cayenne, and salt to taste.
- Mash the avocado all up until you have all the kale bits coated in a lovely creamy sauce.
- Cut the tomatoes in small slices and add them in the bowl.

Nutritional facts:

400 calories Total fat: 30, Sodium: 45mg, Carbs 41g

31. Betterave French Soup

Description:

Beetroots have long been used for medicinal purposes, primarily for disorders of the liver as they help to stimulate the liver's detoxification processes. The plant pigment that gives beetroot its rich, purple-crimson colour is betacyanin; a powerful agent, thought to suppress the development of some types of cancer.

Ingredients:

- 3 tablespoons olive oil
- 1 medium onion, chopped
- 3 cloves garlic, chopped
- 6 medium beets, peeled and chopped
- 2 cups beef stock
- salt and freshly ground pepper
- heavy cream

How to prepare:

- Warm olive oil in a large saucepan over medium heat. Stir in onions and garlic; cook until soft but

- not browned, about 5 minutes. Stir in beets, and cook for 1 minute.
- Stir in stock, and season with salt and pepper. Bring to a boil; cover, and simmer until the beets are tender, about 20 to 30 minutes. Remove from heat, and allow to cool slightly.
- In batches, add soup to a food processor, and pulse until liquefied. Return soup to saucepan, and gently heat through. Ladle into bowls, and garnish with a swirl of cream.

Nutritional facts:

Calories 31, Carbs 5g, Fat 1g, Protein 1g, Sodium 22mg, Sugar 3g

32. Premium Squash Noodles

Description:

Squash is an excellent source of Vitamin A. The so called 'noodles' will be tossed with feta cheese and vegetables. This is one of the easiest way to cook squash.

Ingredients:

- 1 spaghetti squash, halved and seeded
- 2 tbsp vegetable oil
- 1 chopped onion
- ¾ cup crumbled feta cheese
- 1 Minced garlic clove
- 1 ½ cups chopped tomatoes
- 3 tablespoons sliced black olives
- 2 tablespoons chopped basil

How to prepare:

- Preheat oven to 350 degrees F (175 degrees C). Lightly grease a baking sheet..
- Place spaghetti squash with cut sides down on the prepared baking sheet, and bake 30 minutes

in the preheated oven, or until a sharp knife can be inserted with only a little resistance. Remove squash from oven and set aside to cool enough to be easily handled.

- Meanwhile, heat oil in a skillet over medium heat. Cook and stir onion in oil until tender. Add garlic; cook and stir until fragrant, 2 to 3 minutes. Stir in tomatoes and cook until tomatoes are warmed through.
- Use a large spoon to scoop the stringy pulp from the squash and place in a medium bowl. Toss with the vegetables, feta cheese, olives, and basil. Serve warm.

Nutritional facts:

Calories: 147, carbs 12.8, Fat 9.8, Protein 4.1, sodium 269

33. Anti-inflamatory Turmeric Tea

Description:

Turmeric is a deep orange root from India that is used as a spice in a lot of eastern dishes. It has a wonderfully earthy and exotic flavor along with many health benefits: Turmeric has strong anti-oxidant properties that may help prevent cancer. Turmeric is also one of the most potent natural anti-inflammatories. It may help with sprains, strains and other issues related to inflammation.

Ingredients:

- 32 oz boiling water
- ½ Tbsp turmeric powder
- 1 Tbsp fresh ginger, thinly sliced
- 1 handful cilantro, chopped
- 1 garlic clove, peeled and crushed
- 1 Tbsp olive oil
- 2 lemons, juiced
- 5 peppercorns, whole (if tolerated on AIP)
- 1 orange, juiced (or substitute 1½ tbsp honey)

How to prepare:

- Put water on the stove to boil. Combine all ingredients in a strainer or teapot.
- Pour boiling water into the pot and steep for 10 minutes. Strain and enjoy!

Nutritional facts:

Calories 96, Carbs 16g, Fat 4g, Protein 4g, Sodium 12mg

34. Peanut Butter Yogurt Dip

Description:

A wonderfully balanced dip with organic yogurt, cinnamon, peanut butter and honey as a sweetener. Great dip for apples, bananas, graham crackers.

Ingredients:

- 1/2 cup organic whole plain yogurt
- 2-3 Tablespoons all natural peanut butter
- 1 teaspoon vanilla extract
- 2 teaspoons organic honey
- 1 teaspoon cinnamon

How to prepare:

- Combine all ingredients in a small bowl and whisk until combined.
- Serve with apples, bananas, graham crackers, celery or fruit/veggie desired.
- Store any remaining dip in a small container and refrigerate.

Nutritional facts:

Per Serving: 60.2 calories, 3.1 gr fat, 36 mg sodium, 5.9 gr carbs, .6 gr fiber, 5.0 gr sugar, 2.0 gr protein

35. Avocado's Madness

Description:

Avocados are rich in cancer-fighting carotenoids, which are most plentiful in the dark-green portion of the flesh that's closest to the skin •

Ingredients:

- 1 avocado - peeled, pitted and diced
- 1 lime, juiced
- 1 mango - peeled, seeded and diced
- 1 small red onion, chopped
- 1 habanero pepper, seeded and chopped
- 1 tablespoon chopped fresh cilantro •

How to prepare:

- Place the avocado in a serving bowl, and mix with the lime juice.
- Mix in the mango, onion, habanero pepper, cilantro and salt.

Nutritional facts:

Calories: 252, Carbs 33, Fats: 15, Protein: 3, Sodium: 204, Sugars: 0

36. Fresh Morning Salad

Description:

A simple spinach salad special by adding avocado, spices and fresh cilantro. Make it ahead, refrigerate and then toss right before serving.

Ingredients:

- 3 tablespoons fresh lime juice
- 3 tablespoons olive oil
- 1 tablespoon chopped fresh cilantro
- 1 teaspoon sugar
- 1/4 teaspoon ground cumin
- 1/4 teaspoon kosher salt
- 1/8 teaspoon black pepper
- 1 Hass avocado, peeled, pitted and thinly sliced
- 1 small red onion, thinly sliced
- 11 ounces baby spinach

How to prepare:

- Whisk lime juice, oil, cilantro, sugar, cumin, salt and pepper in a large serving bowl.

- Stir in avocado and red onion.
- Lay spinach on top. (Salad can be prepared and refrigerated up to 2 hours ahead.) Toss just before serving.

Nutritional facts:

Calories: 99, Fats: 9, Carbs: 5, Sodium 93

37. Green Beans Sticks

Description:

Rich in antioxidants and detoxifying nutrients, green beans contain fiber and chlorophyll (which both act as entire body purifiers and protectors), antioxidants, amino acids, folate (that converts to folic acid), vitamin A, and vitamin C

Ingredients:

- 2 pounds green beans, ends trimmed
- 3 tablespoon extra-virgin olive oil
- 2 large garlic cloves, minced
- 1 teaspoon red pepper flakes
- 1 tablespoon lemon zest
- Salt and freshly ground black pepper

How to prepare:

- Blanch green beans in a large stock pot of well salted boiling water until bright green in color and tender crisp, roughly 2 minutes. Drain and shock in a bowl of ice water to stop from cooking.

- Heat a large heavy skillet over medium heat. Add the oil. Add the garlic and red pepper flakes and saute until fragrant, about 30 seconds. Add the beans and continue to saute about 5 minutes. Add lemon zest and season with salt and pepper.

Nutritional facts:

Calories: 366, Fats: 27, Protein: 2

38. Modern Cauliflower Steaks

Description:

Add some color to your cauliflower with turmeric. These cauliflower steaks are easy to prepare and would make an excellent vegetarian side or main dish. Turmeric contains 2-5% curcumin as one of the most important component in it. Curcumin plays an important role in slowing down skin cancer which occurs due to over exposure to ultraviolet rays in the sunlight.

Ingredients:

- 1 large (about 1.2kg) cauliflower
- 1/4 cup extra virgin olive oil, plus extra for frying
- 1 teaspoon ground turmeric
- Fried curry leaves, to serve
- Thinly sliced fried red chilli, to serve

How to prepare:

- Preheat oven to 180C/160C fan forced. Line 2 baking trays with foil.
- Cut the cauliflower into four 1.5cm-thick slices,

leaving base intact. Cook steaks in extra virgin olive oil in a non-stick frying pan over medium-high heat for 2-3 minutes each side or until golden. Transfer to the foil-lined baking tray.

- Whisk the olive oil with the turmeric in a bowl until combined. Brush over steaks.
- Roast cauliflower in the oven for 12-15 minutes or until tender and crisp.
- Scatter with fried curry leaves and thinly sliced red chilli, to serve.

Nutritional facts:

Calories: 161, Carbs 7, Fats: 15, Protein: 2.4, Sodium: 30.8, Sugars: 0.1

39. Asparagus Saves the Day

Description:

Asparagus is a very good source of fiber, folate, vitamins A, C, E and K, as well as chromium, a trace mineral that enhances the ability of insulin to transport glucose from the bloodstream into cells

Ingredients:

- 1 bunch asparagus (about 3/4 pound), ends trimmed
- 1 tablespoon olive oil
- ¼ cup chopped walnuts
- 1 garlic clove, minced
- ½ teaspoon chopped fresh thymeleaves, preferably lemon thyme
- 1 ounce Parmesan, finely grated (1/4 cup)
- Kosher salt, as needed
- ¼ teaspoon black pepper

How to prepare:

- First thing is to steam the asparagus.

- Stir in the nuts and cook until fragrant, about 2 minutes. Stir in the garlic and thyme and cook until fragrant, about 30 seconds. Remove from heat and whisk in the cheese. Season with salt and pepper. Spoon nut mixture over warm asparagus and serve at once.

Nutritional facts:

134 calories; 11 grams fat; 4 protein, 100 mg sodium, 4g carbs

40. Shrimps gone Wild

Description:

Shrimp are supercharged with vitamin B12 and selenium. In addition, they provide a fair amount of vitamin A, vitamin E, vitamin B6, iron, magnesium, sodium (salt), zinc and copper. Surprisingly, they also contain some vitamin C

Ingredients:

- 1 pound wild caught large shrimp (peeled and deveined)
- Juice of ½ of a fresh lemon
- 3 tablespoon olive oil
- ¼ tsp black pepper
- ¼ tsp unrefined sea salt

How to prepare:

- Preheat the grill to medium heat.
- Place the shrimp onto the skewers.
- In a small saucepan. Squeeze lemon juice into the mixture and stir well.
- Put the shrimp onto the greased grill and baste

generously with lemon mixture. Cook for 4-5 minutes and then turn.
- Baste other side of shrimp and cook for another 4-5 minutes or until the shrimp turns pink and is cooked through.
- Serve shrimp over a bed of red quinoa.

Nutritional facts:

Calories: 230, Fat: 12g, Carbs: 0g, Protein: 27g

41. Quinoa and its Friends

Description:

Protein-packed quinoa is toasted, then cooked until tender with sweet peppers and garlic for a hearty side dish. You can serve this wholesome grain dish hot, at room temperature or even chilled--perfect for any season.

Ingredients:

- 1 tablespoon olive oil
- 1 shallot, minced
- 2 cloves garlic, minced
- 1 medium red bell pepper, diced
- 1 medium yellow bell pepper, diced
- 1 cup uncooked quinoa, rinsed
- 2 cups Swanson
- 2 tablespoons chopped fresh parsley

How to prepare:

- Heat the oil in a 2-quart saucepan over medium-high heat. Add the shallot and garlic and cook for 2 minutes, stirring occasionally. Add the peppers

and quinoa and cook for 2 minutes, stirring occasionally.
- Stir in the broth and heat to a boil. Reduce the heat to low. Cover and cook for 20 minutes or until the quinoa is tender and the liquid is absorbed. Stir in the parsley. Season, if desired.

Nutritional facts:

Calories: 223 kcal, Fat: 6.1 g, Carbs: 35.2g, Protein: 7.1 g, Sodium: 272 mg

42. Trusty Watercress Salad

Description:

Watercress, which makes a nice addition to salads and sandwiches, is an anti-cancer food par excellence. Research suggests that eating fresh watercress daily can significantly reduce blood cell DNA damage. DNA damage in blood cells is an indicator of a person's overall cancer risk. Watercress contains a special mustard oil called phenethyl isothiocyanate which has significant cancer fighting powers.

Ingredients:

- tablespoons fresh lime juice
- 1 teaspoon white sugar
- 1 teaspoon minced fresh ginger root
- 1/4 cup vegetable oil
- 2 bunches watercress, trimmed and chopped
- 2 1/2 cups cubed watermelon
- 2 1/2 cups cubed cantaloupe
- 1/3 cup toasted and sliced almonds

How to prepare:

- In a large bowl, whisk together lime juice, sugar, and ginger. Gradually add oil and season with salt and pepper to taste.
- Add watercress, watermelon, and cantaloupe to dressing and toss to coat. Transfer salad to plates, sprinkle with sliced almonds and serve immediately.

Nutritional facts:

Calories 274 Fat: 20 Carbs: 21 Protein 6.9 Sodium 69

43. Crunchy Cherries

Description:

Cherries are naturally rich in perillyl alcohol (POH), a compound that has been found to be effective at destroying cancer cells in vitro and in vivo. Cherry pie filling is lovingly sandwiched between 2 layers of crunchy oaty goodness. Substitute apple pie filling and sprinkle a little extra cinnamon over the top if you like.

Ingredients:

- 1 cup rolled oats
- 1 cup all-purpose flour
- 3/4 cup brown sugar
- 1/2 teaspoon ground cinnamon
- 2 tablespoon olive oil
- 1 (21 ounce) can cherry pie filling

How to prepare:

- Preheat oven to 375 degrees F (190 degrees C.)
- In a medium bowl, combine the rolled oats, flour, brown sugar and cinnamon.

- Sprinkle one half of crumb mixture in the bottom of a 9 inch square baking dish. Cover with cherry pie filling. Sprinkle remaining crumb mixture over pie filling.
- Bake in the preheated oven for 40 minutes, or until topping is golden brown. Serve warm.

Nutritional facts:

Calories 321, fat: 11, carbs: 53, Protein: 3, Sodium: 91

ADDITIONAL TITLES FROM THIS AUTHOR

70 Effective Meal Recipes to Prevent and Solve Being Overweight: Burn Fat Fast by Using Proper Dieting and Smart Nutrition

By

Joe Correa CSN

48 Acne Solving Meal Recipes: The Fast and Natural Path to Fixing Your Acne Problems in Less Than 10 Days!

By

Joe Correa CSN

41 Alzheimer's Preventing Meal Recipes: Reduce or Eliminate Your Alzheimer's Condition in 30 Days or Less!

By

Joe Correa CSN

70 Effective Breast Cancer Meal Recipes: Prevent and Fight Breast Cancer with Smart Nutrition and Powerful Foods

By

Joe Correa CSN

www.ingramcontent.com/pod-product-compliance
Lightning Source LLC
Chambersburg PA
CBHW070443090526
44586CB00046B/1976